Looking Back

THE NIAGARA RIVER

THE ONTARIO SHORE

Dedicated to The Niagara Parks Commission which, since 1885, has preserved and enhanced the natural beauty of Niagara Falls and the Niagara River corridor.

Looking Back

THE NIAGARA RIVER
THE ONTARIO SHORE

Sherman Zavitz

Looking Back Press

Vanwell Publishing acknowledges the financial support of the Government of Canada through the Book Publishing Industry Development Program for our publishing activities.

Published by Looking Back Press
An Imprint of Vanwell Publishing Limited
1 Northrup Crescent, P.O. Box 2131
St. Catharines, ON L2R 7S2
For all general information contact Looking Back Press at:
Telephone 905-937-3100 ext. 829
Fax 905-937-1760
E-Mail vanessa.mclean@vanwell.com

For customer service and orders:
Toll-free 1-800-661-6136

Printed in Canada

National Library of Canada Cataloguing in Publication

Zavitz, Sherman, 1940-
    The Niagara River : the Ontario shore / Sherman Zavitz.

(Looking back)
ISBN 1-55068-955-X

    1. Niagara River (N.Y. and Ont.)—History—Pictorial works.
  2. Niagara
Falls Region (Ont.)—History—Pictorial works. I. Title. II. Series: Looking back
(St. Catharines, Ont.)

FC3095.N5Z394 2006
                                971.3'38
                    C2006-906469-5

Contents

Acknowledgements

My sincere thanks to those individuals who have helped so significantly to make this book a reality. They are: Shawn Fleming, Information Services Librarian at the Fort Erie Public Library; Andrew Porteus, Manager of Adult Reference and Information Services, Niagara Falls, Ontario Public Library; Kevin Windsor, Curator of the Lundy's Lane Historical Museum, Niagara Falls, Ontario; Clark Bernat, Managing Director of the Niagara Historical Society and Museum, Niagara-on-the-Lake; and Sarah Byers-Ogilvie, Curator, and Scott Nicholson, Assistant Curator, both of the Willoughby Historical Museum, Niagara Falls, Ontario.

Thanks also to Rebecca Pascoe of The Niagara Parks Commission for information about the McFarland House.

My wife, Ann, was not only a source of encouragement but was quite willing to spend many hours at the computer keyboard. My son, Michael, also willingly provided support and technical assistance.

I am grateful once again to Ben Kooter, President of Vanwell Publishing Limited and Vanessa McLean, Managing Editor of Looking Back Press, an imprint of Vanwell Publishing. Their support of this type of endeavour is commendable.

Introduction

The Niagara River is among the most famous and most visited waterways in the world. The river, more correctly a strait connecting Lakes Erie and Ontario, wears many faces during its 35-mile (56km) run. You can see rapids, a whirlpool, wide peaceful stretches, a gorge and, of course, waterfalls. For most of the millions of visitors who descend on Niagara each year, the Falls are the focal point. They are among nature's most spectacular and sublime creations. For many generations, Niagara's tumbling torrents and roaring rapids have inspired and fascinated.

The river, straddling the border of Ontario and New York State, has a long and fascinating history. Through the use of over170 old photos and engravings, mostly from the late nineteenth and early twentieth century, this volume depicts some of the beautiful scenery and heritage along the Canadian side of the Niagara. In these pages you will find many aspects of life as it once was in the various communities along the river's west bank. Most of the images used relate to various themes of Niagara's heritage – recreation, tourism, hydroelectric power, stunters and bridges, as well as the military, including of course, the War of 1812.

Come, then, for a photographic journey down the Niagara from its entrance at Lake Erie to its mouth at Lake Ontario, as we present some sights from yesteryear.

Sherman Zavitz
Niagara Falls, Ontario
September 2006

The Niagara River Communities

Fort Erie

Fort Erie is located at the entrance to the Niagara River at Lake Erie, opposite Buffalo, New York. The British first constructed a fort at this strategic point in 1764. The community that eventually developed in the immediate area took the name of the fortification. By the end of the War of 1812, the fort was in ruins. It was reconstructed in the late 1930s and has since become an important tourist attraction.

Beginning in the 1870s, Fort Erie became a major rail centre, helped in large measure by the opening of the International Railway Bridge across the Niagara River in 1873. The building of the Peace Bridge, which was dedicated in 1927, further strengthened Fort Erie's position as an important and busy crossing point for trade and travel between Canada and the United States.

Black Creek

Located about halfway between Fort Erie and Niagara Falls, the creek received its name from the dark colour of its water. Beginning in the 1790s, a small pioneer community developed around the mouth of the creek where it flows into the Niagara River. Today, Black Creek is part of the Municipality of Greater Fort Erie.

Chippawa

The picturesque village of Chippawa was founded in the early 1790s at the mouth of Chippawa Creek, where it emptied into the Niagara River. From 1790 until 1830, when the Welland Canal opened for its first season, Chippawa was the southern terminus of the Portage Road, a vital transportation artery that was used to bypass the rapids and falls of the Niagara River. Incorporated in 1850, Chippawa was an important shipbuilding and industrial centre during the mid-1800s. It amalgamated with the City of Niagara Falls in 1970.

Niagara Falls

The city of Niagara Falls, Ontario, was created in 1904 following the amalgamation of two early adjacent communities. Additional amalgamations have taken place in subsequent years. Tourism has been of major importance to the city's economy for many decades. However, other factors such as the international bridges crossing the Niagara River, major rail lines, and a number of early hydroelectric power plants also contributed significantly to the city's development. In the early decades of the twentieth century many manufacturing industries located in Niagara Falls, lured there by the proximity of plentiful and inexpensive electricity. As one of the most visited cities in the world, Niagara Falls offers an enormous number and variety of attractions.

Queenston

A pretty village at the base of the Niagara Escarpment, this early community was first known as The Queen's Town, in recognition of The Queen's Own Rangers who had their barracks there. By the early 1800s, the name Queenston was in more common use. Although it resulted in the death of the much-admired Isaac Brock, the Battle of Queenston Heights on October 13, 1812, was a significant victory for the British and Canadians.

As the northern terminus of the Portage Road, Queenston prospered as a trans-shipment point until the Welland Canal opened in 1830 for its first full season. Queenston is now part of the Municipality of Niagara-on-the-Lake.

Niagara-on-the-Lake

One of the best preserved early nineteenth century towns in North America, Niagara-on-the-Lake was originally settled in the 1780s by Loyalist refugees from the United States. From 1791 to 1796, it was the first capital of what is now the Province of Ontario. Captured and burned by the Americans in 1813 during the War of 1812, the town was rebuilt shortly after.

Niagara-on-the-Lake's beautiful setting at the mouth of the Niagara River where it meets Lake Ontario, its lovely landscaped streets and parks, the abundance of restored heritage buildings and the presence of the renowned Shaw Festival all combine to create a special charm and atmosphere few communities can match.

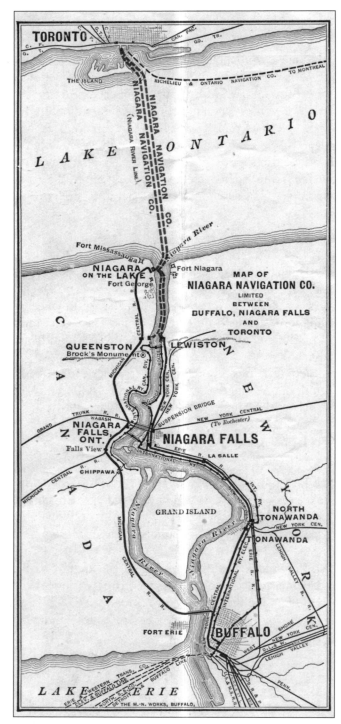

This 1907 map of the Niagara River shows the various rail lines and steamship routes then in use.

One
Fort Erie

Ferry service between Fort Erie and Buffalo existed for more than 150 years. Traffic, both auto and horse-drawn, gathers at the ferry landing at the foot of Bertie Street in this photo from 1908. The *Hope* may be seen at the dock. The large building at the right was the customs office. At one time there were many ferry landings in Fort Erie. However, the Bertie Street dock lasted the longest. It was in use from around 1796 to 1950. (Sherman Zavitz Collection)

The ferryboat *Niagara Frontier*, seen here at the Bertie Street landing about 1910, had a capacity of 40 cars. Crossing the Niagara River took about 20 minutes. (Sherman Zavitz Collection)

A remarkable engineering achievement for the time, the International Railway Bridge across the Niagara River opened on November 3, 1873. One of Canada's most out-standing civil engineers, Casimir Gzowski, was in charge of the project. The bridge contributed significantly to the growth in trade between Canada and the United States. It also turned Fort Erie and Buffalo into major railroad centres. This double view dates to around 1906. (Sherman Zavitz Collection)

A herd of cattle takes a refreshing dip in the Niagara River in this picture from 1905. Part of the Buffalo skyline may be seen in the background. (Sherman Zavitz Collection)

The ferry *City of Toledo* in the Niagara River at Fort Erie. Built in 1891, it was scrapped in 1948. (Francis J. Petrie Collection, Niagara Falls (Ontario) Public Library)

Niagara Street (now the Niagara Boulevard) near its intersection with Bertie Street presents a busy appearance in this photo taken around 1915. The King Edward Hotel is on the right. (Niagara Falls Public Library)

WATER FRONT, FORT ERIE, ONT.

The Fort Erie waterfront from the Niagara River around 1925. The Bertie Street ferry landing can be seen in the distance. Note the high transmission tower at the left. (Niagara Falls Public Library)

The first Fort Erie was constructed in 1764 on the Lake Erie shore, close to the Niagara River's entrance. This painting of the fort by Edward Walsh was made in 1804 by which time the fort had suffered a significant amount of storm and erosion damage. That same year work began on a new fort a short distance away on higher ground. The hunters are shooting wild pigeons. (Niagara Falls Public Library)

Fort Erie saw considerable action during the War of 1812. The fort was occupied by American forces from July 3, 1814 until November 5 that year, when they destroyed it and retreated across the river to Buffalo.

Fort Erie remained a ruin for many years. The site came under the ownership of The Niagara Parks Commission in 1901. Beginning in 1937, a reconstruction of the fort was begun, using funds from a joint provincial-federal government program. The resurrected fort was opened to the public on July 1, 1939. (Niagara Falls Public Library)

The Fort Erie Racetrack is one of the oldest in North America. The first meet began on June 16, 1897. This 1908 photo shows part of the track and, in the distance, the original grandstand. (Sherman Zavitz Collection)

Before the International Railway Bridge was opened in 1873, railway cars had to be ferried across the Niagara River. (Fort Erie Public Library)

Construction of the Peace Bridge across the Niagara River at Fort Erie began in August 1925. (Fort Erie Public Library)

Although the Peace Bridge opened for traffic on June 1, 1927, the official opening was held on August 7 that year. Thousands gathered for the occasion. Among the dignitaries present were H.R.H. Edward, Prince of Wales and his brother, Prince George. (Fort Erie Public Library)

The Peace Bridge is a key artery between the United States and Canada and a symbol of enduring friendship between the two countries. This photo is from the 1930s. (Fort Erie Public Library)

This grist mill was built in 1792 along the Niagara River in the area of the present-day Peace Bridge. It was destroyed by fire in 1861. (Fort Erie Public Library)

An interesting sketch of the Fort Erie riverfront, circa 1870. (Fort Erie Public Library)

Along the Niagara River near Fort Erie in the 1920s. (Fort Erie Public Library)

"White Hall" Club House, Bridgeburg.

The White Hall Clubhouse along the Niagara River in the early 1900s. (Fort Erie Public Library)

Willie's Dock was a popular swimming spot on the Niagara River during the 1920s. (Fort Erie Public Library)

Two
Fort Erie to Black Creek

The Cozy Dell along the Niagara River in the 1920s. (Fort Erie Public Library)

Fort Erie and N. Boulevard, Fort Erie, Can.

This is what the road along the Niagara River near Fort Erie looked like in the early years of the twentieth century. (Sherman Zavitz Collection)

Seward Cary began carrying passengers on his "coach and four" between Buffalo, Fort Erie and Niagara Falls in 1893. Known as the Red Jacket or the Tally-Ho, the coach was painted green with black and scarlet trim. Cary, as the driver, wore a high green beaver hat and a long green coat. The coach is seen here near Black Creek. Tally-Ho service ended in 1902. (Fort Erie Public Library)

In 1903 construction began on the Canadian Ship Building Company's yard along the Niagara River, where the Niagara Parks Marina is now. The first ship to be built at this yard was the *E.B. Osler,* seen here being launched on September 7, 1907. The shipyard, which was closed at various times and had several owners, ended operations in 1920. (Fort Erie Public Library)

The original part of this house, among the oldest along the Niagara River, was built around 1805 by Ulrich Strickler. It was enlarged by Joseph Danner about 1820. In 1855, the house was purchased by Elias Sherk. It was still in the Sherk family when this picture was taken in 1876. The residence still stands. (Fort Erie Public Library)

A charming scene along the upper Niagara River around 1900. Grand Island is in the background. (City of Niagara Falls, Ont. Museums, Willoughby Historical Museum)

Navy Island from the Canadian side as depicted by the excellent nineteenth century topographical artist William Henry Bartlett. The engraving was originally published in 1842. This uninhabited island, Canadian territory, about three miles above the Falls (5km), is a nature reserve. It received its name during the 1760s when the British had a shipyard on the island. Here, a number of ships were built for the Royal Navy's use on the upper Great Lakes. (City of Niagara Falls, Ont. Museums, Willoughby Historical Museum)

H.R.H. Edward, Prince of Wales (later King Edward VIII) was driven along the Niagara River from Fort Erie to Niagara Falls on August 7, 1927. Here, the Prince is crossing the bridge at Black Creek. (City of Niagara Falls, Ont. Museums, Willoughby Historical Museum)

An 1890s scene at the mouth of Black Creek with the Niagara River at the extreme left. (City of Niagara Falls, Ont. Museums, Willoughby Historical Museum)

Canoeists out for a paddle on Black Creek, close to where it empties into the Niagara River, circa 1900. The railway trestle across the creek and the Black Creek station can be seen at the right. (City of Niagara Falls, Ont. Museums, Willoughby Historical Museum)

Bridge over Ushers Creek, Canadian Niagara Boulevard, near Niagara Falls, Canada.

The picturesque bridge and surroundings at Ussher's Creek about 1915. The Niagara River is at the left. (Francis J. Petrie Collection, Niagara Falls Public Library)

This is a view of the mouth of Street's Creek, or Ussher's Creek as it is now called, from 1860. Looking north, the Niagara River is to the right. The area beyond the bridge was the site of the Battle of Chippawa, July 5, 1814, one of the significant land battles of the War of 1812. The Canadians and British under Major General Phineas Riall were defeated by the American army commanded by Major General Jacob Brown. Some American historians characterize this battle as the birth of the American army, since it was the first time U.S. soldiers met and defeated British regulars in open battle on level ground. (*Lossing's Pictorial Field Book of the War of 1812*)

Slater's Dock as it looked in 1896. This facility was along the Niagara River about a mile and a half above Chippawa. Using the electric line railway from Niagara Falls, passengers could connect here with the steamboat to Buffalo. The Slater home, known as Willoughby Grove, may be seen at the extreme left. Boat service from Slater's Dock ended in the fall of 1905. (City of Niagara Falls, Ont. Museums, Willoughby Historical Museum)

Three
Chippawa

The *Erie Belle* was one of the last sailing ships on the Great Lakes. It is seen here, abandoned, around 1910 at the Chippawa dock close to the Niagara River. (City of Niagara Falls, Ont. Museums, Willoughby Historical Museum)

This lovely scene, which dates to about 1915, shows the lighthouse at the junction of the Niagara River and Chippawa Creek. The picture was taken by Ernest Fox, a local photographer at that time. The channel in the foreground was dug about 1829 to make it easier for ships entering or leaving the creek. The island that was created became known as Hog Island. It no longer exists. The car is travelling along what is now the Niagara Parkway. (Frank and Patricia Foley, Niagara Falls Public Library)

This view of Chippawa was taken about 1920 from the top of the water tower, which stood where the Chippawa Branch Library is now. The roof of the Town Hall is in the lower right corner. The southern portion of Cummington Square and its bandstand are visible. Main Street can be seen stretching east towards the Niagara River at the top of the picture. (Don Ede Collection)

An early twentieth century look at Cummington Square, Chippawa. All the buildings, with the exception of the one at the extreme left, still stand. (Sherman Zavitz Collection)

It's a hot summer's day around 1910 and a game of water baseball is underway on Chippawa Creek. Looking carefully, you can see that the pitcher has just thrown the ball. The bridge shown was constructed in 1894 and was replaced in 1919. (Sherman Zavitz Collection)

The mouth of Chippawa Creek as it flows into the Niagara River, depicted in *Picturesque Canada*, 1882. (Sherman Zavitz Collection)

The Laura Secord House at Chippawa. Laura, a War of 1812 hero, lived here as a widow from 1841 until her passing in 1868. She was 93. (Niagara Historical Society and Museum)

The railway trestle across Chippawa Creek at Chippawa in 1906. The station is the building right of centre with two windows in the end wall. Note the many boathouses on the far side of the creek. (Sherman Zavitz Collection)

The Niagara River, with the entrance to Chippawa Creek visible at the far right, where the Hog Island Lighthouse may also be seen. A portion of a tourist accommodation establishment called the Old Manor Camp is in the background. (Sherman Zavitz Collection)

Four
Niagara Falls

The title of this 1905 photo reads "Autumn beauties along Niagara's precipitous banks looking up towards the Falls." (Sherman Zavitz Collection)

Dating to about 1870, this image shows a top-hatted gentleman viewing the Falls from a rocky outcrop known as Victoria Point. (Sherman Zavitz Collection)

Table Rock presents a fantastic winter show in the 1870s. The Horseshoe Falls and the Canadian shoreline are in the background. (Sherman Zavitz Collection)

Following the close of the 1860 tourist season at the Falls, the *Maid of the Mist* steamboat was sold. A Montreal firm purchased the craft on condition it be delivered down the river to Lake Ontario. This meant attempting something that had never been done – taking a boat through the extremely dangerous lower rapids and whirlpool of the Niagara River. Amazingly, on June 6, 1861, with Capt. Joel Robinson at the helm, the trip was successfully made. Here, the *Maid* is crashing through the rapids. The Lower Suspension Bridge is in the background. (Sherman Zavitz Collection)

Cedar Island, seen here in the 1860s, was directly above the Horseshoe Falls and was connected to the mainland by a bridge. The observation tower on the island was known as Street's Pagoda. In 1904, during construction for the Canadian Niagara Power Plant, the channel between the mainland and the island was filled in. (Sherman Zavitz Collection)

The Upper Suspension Bridge was opened in 1869. This picture from the mid-1870s shows a maintenance crew at work. Several men are standing on a narrow platform below the bridge, while another appears to be standing on the railing. In the background, through the maze of wires, is the original Clifton House, Niagara Falls's largest and most famous nineteenth century hotel. It stood where Oakes Garden Theatre is now located. (Sherman Zavitz Collection)

Dressed in their finest, this quartet poses for the camera with the American Falls in the background. (Sherman Zavitz Collection)

Located a short distance above the Horseshoe Falls, two early generating stations, the Canadian Niagara (in the foreground) and the Toronto Power Plant, are seen here around 1915. (Sherman Zavitz Collection)

A spectacular view of the Steel Arch Bridge, which replaced the Lower Suspension Bridge in 1897. Like its predecessor, the Lower Arch Bridge was a double-deck span with trains crossing on the upper level and carriages and pedestrians using the lower deck. This span, now known as the Whirlpool Rapids Bridge, is still in use. (Sherman Zavitz Collection)

King George VI and his wife, Queen Elizabeth view the Falls from Table Rock on June 7, 1939. The King is standing just behind his wife, facing the camera. (Sherman Zavitz Collection)

"Maid of the Mist" Landing, showing Incline Railway and Upper Steel Arch Bridge. Niagara Falls, Ont., Canada

With smoke billowing in its wake, the *Maid of the Mist* moves towards its dock, part of which can be seen at the extreme right of this circa 1910 photo. The 1898 Falls View or Upper Steel Arch Bridge can be seen in the background as well as a number of industries on the New York State side of the river. At the left is the Incline Railway. Built in 1894, it transported passengers down the side of the gorge to the *Maid of the Mist* dock. The fare was 5 cents. (Sherman Zavitz Collection)

Dining by the Falls has always been an extra special experience. These diners from the 1930s are enjoying a meal under the awning of the Victoria Park Restaurant, overlooking the Horseshoe or Canadian Falls. (Sherman Zavitz Collection)

The Falls View Bridge, which replaced the Upper Suspension Bridge, opened in 1898. During January 1938, a monster ice jam in the gorge just below the Falls weakened the bridge's supports so severely that it collapsed onto the ice. These three photos show the bridge just before, during and just after the fall on January 27, 1938. (Sherman Zavitz Collection)

A Michigan Central Railroad train is stopped at the Falls View platform to allow passengers a look at the Falls, circa 1890s. (Sherman Zavitz Collection)

Almost resembling creatures from outer space, these individuals swathed in their oilskins have just boarded the *Maid of the Mist* sightseeing boat. The Horseshoe Falls is in the distance. (Sherman Zavitz Collection)

Mrs. Dam   Miss Dam   Cissy Dam   Baby Dam

Mr. Dam   Master Dam   Kitty Dam   The Dam Dog

THE WHOLE DAM FAMILY AT NIAGARA FALLS

This humorous card from 1905 shows "The Whole Dam Family at Niagara Falls" – including the Dam Dog. (Sherman Zavitz Collection)

View from Niagara Falls Tourist Camp, Niagara Falls Canada. Just up the hill from Clifton Hotel

A number of tents and cabins along with picnic tables and cars can be seen in this view of the Niagara Falls Tourist Camp on Clifton Hill. At the left, just below the camp, you can see the Foxhead Hotel. Built by Howard Fox, this English Tudor style building opened in 1925 and was a landmark hotel in Niagara Falls for many years. The Horseshoe Falls is visible near the upper left corner. (Sherman Zavitz Collection)

The two *Maids of the Mist* resting at their docks around 1920. The first Maid began operating in 1846 as a ferryboat, taking passengers back and forth across the Niagara River just below the Falls. Two years later, after the opening of the first Suspension Bridge, the *Maid of the Mist* became a sightseeing boat, offering visitors an exhilarating and memorable close-up view of the Falls. Today, a small fleet of Maids continues to provide what a mid-nineteenth century writer described as "the most wonderful water trip in the world." (Sherman Zavitz Collection)

A lovely painting of Niagara Falls from around 1900. The imposing Loretto Academy can be seen in the background, overlooking the Horseshoe Falls. Founded in 1861, Loretto operated for many years as a girls' school as well as a convent. The facility closed in 2005. Looking closely, you can also see a train just below Loretto and the *Maid of the Mist* approaching the Horseshoe Falls. (Sherman Zavitz Collection)

Flags are flying as the Spanish Aero Car makes its inaugural run across the Whirlpool on August 8, 1916. Originally operated by a private Spanish company, this popular attraction is now owned by The Niagara Parks Commission. (Sherman Zavitz Collection)

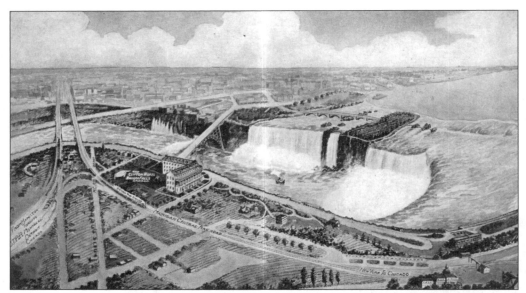

An advertising card from about 1915 for the second Clifton Hotel. (Sherman Zavitz Collection)

Niagara Falls, Canada, Works of the Ontario Power Co. from Goat Island

This photo of the Ontario Power Company's generating station was taken not long after it opened in 1905. The large building on the high bank was the company's distribution station. This is where the Niagara Fallsview Casino and Resort is now located. The Ontario Power Company's plant, later owned by Ontario Hydro, ceased operations in 1999. (Sherman Zavitz Collection)

A dramatic depiction of the collapse of Table Rock, June 26, 1850. As can be seen, a driver who was washing his omnibus on the rock at the time barely escaped with his life. The Horseshoe Falls is in the background. A prominent shelf some 200 feet (61m) long, Table Rock had been a well-known observation platform. Most of what was left following the collapse was blasted off in 1935 for safety reasons. (Sherman Zavitz Collection)

These two aerial views, one taken from just above the Falls and the other just below, were made in 1920. (Sherman Zavitz Collection)

Clifford Calverly performs on the tightrope across the Niagara Gorge in 1892. The Lower Suspension Bridge is doubling as a grandstand. (Sherman Zavitz Collection)

The Scenic Tunnel under the Horseshoe Falls as seen in 1930. This popular attraction is now known as Journey Behind the Falls. (Sherman Zavitz Collection)

This is the view of the Falls that guests of the Clifton Hotel had from the hotel's piazza (or verandah) in 1908. The Clifton was situated where Oakes Garden Theatre is now. (Sherman Zavitz Collection)

An artist's rendition of the impressive Electrical Development Company's generating station just above the Horseshoe Falls. Later known as the Toronto Powerhouse, this plant opened in 1906 and was closed in 1974. (Sherman Zavitz Collection)

In 1899 lawn tennis courts were established in Queen Victoria Park opposite the American Falls. The Niagara Parks Commission no longer offers recreational facilities in Queen Victoria Park, but does maintain tennis courts at Queenston Heights Park. (Sherman Zavitz Collection)

At one time large company picnics were very common in Queen Victoria Park. This photo was taken during the Hamilton Grocers' Picnic held during the summer of 1906. Looking closely, you can see that the large crowd is watching some foot races. Queen Victoria Park, the park by the Falls, was opened to the public on May 24 (the Queen's birthday), 1888.(Sherman Zavitz Collection)

Taken in July 1920, this view is looking north along River Road (the Niagara Parkway) from the foot of Clifton Hill. The second Clifton Hotel is on the corner, while the Lafayette Hotel can be seen in the distance. A portion of the Falls View Bridge is also visible. The four box-like towers belonged to the Pittsburgh Reduction Company on the New York State side of the river. (Sherman Zavitz Collection)

The first span across the Niagara River was this wooden suspension bridge, which opened on August 1, 1848. It was located where the Whirlpool Rapids Bridge is now. This original bridge was replaced by a double deck structure on the same site. It was built between 1853 and 1855. (Niagara Falls Public Library)

Dwarfed by giant icicles, this couple is about to begin a wintertime trek under the Horseshoe Falls, part of which can be seen in the background. The photo dates to 1905. (Sherman Zavitz Collection)

This is an 1870s view of Niagara Falls's earliest tourist attraction. Known as the Burning Spring, it was located where Dufferin Islands are now. The Niagara River is at the left. The Burning Spring was a natural gas vent along the river's shoreline. (Niagara Falls Heritage Foundation Niagara Falls Public Library)

A barrel with a pipe protruding from the top was placed over the vent. A cork stopper was then put in the pipe. When a crowd gathered and had paid their admission fees, the cork was removed allowing the gas to escape. The gas was then ignited, creating a "burning spring." (Sherman Zavitz Collection)

A train chugs along the edge of the high bank above the Falls in the 1870s. (Sherman Zavitz Collection)

Jean Lussier triumphantly stands on top of his large innovative rubber ball just after going over the Horseshoe Falls inside the sphere. It was July 4, 1928. The ball, which weighed 760 pounds (345kg), had a double steel-band framework and was lined with interconnected rubber sacs filled with oxygen. He later sold pieces of the tubes from the ball's inner lining for 50 cents a cut. (Sherman Zavitz Collection)

It is the night of December 29, 1837, and the steamer *Caroline,* ablaze from bow to stern, is about to slip over the Horseshoe Falls. There was nobody on board. This incident came about during the closing days of the Upper Canada Rebellion of 1837. A number of Canadian rebels (or Patriots as they called themselves) had established a camp on Navy Island, Canadian territory about three miles above the Falls. Intent on forcing a change in the way the British ruled Canada, these men and their American sympathizers were being supplied by an American vessel, the *Caroline,* from the U.S. mainland. On the night of December 29, a force of Canadian volunteers crossed the Niagara River from Chippawa to the American side, cut the *Caroline* loose, torched it and set it adrift. In reality, the ship broke up before reaching the Falls. (Francis J. Petrie Collection, Niagara Falls Public Library)

The Battle of Lundy's Lane took place on July 25, 1814. Fought only about a mile from the Falls at the eastern end of William Lundy's long laneway, it was a particularly brutal, bloody contest. The battle began about 7pm. By around midnight both exhausted armies had fought each other to a standstill. The Americans then withdrew to their camp at Chippawa, leaving the British in possession of the field – and their cannon, which the Americans had previously captured. The battle was a strategic victory for the British since the Americans never again launched a major offensive in the Niagara area. Benson Lossing sketched this portion of the battlefield, which included a Presbyterian Meeting House, in 1860. A portion of what is now called Drummond Hill Cemetery may also be seen. (*Lossing's Pictorial Field Book of the War of 1812*)

Safety procedures and equipment are nowhere in sight as crib work construction gets underway for the Electrical Development Company's power plant on September 3, 1903. (Niagara Falls Public Library)

In the 1920s, a summer swim at Dufferin Islands was very popular. Consisting of 13 little islands, this quiet backwater or embayment of the Niagara River is located a short distance above the Horseshoe Falls. The islands are named for an early Governor General of Canada, Lord Dufferin. (Niagara Falls Public Library)

Maria Spelterini, wearing peach baskets on her feet, performs on a tightrope across the Niagara River Gorge during July 1876. Upriver towards the Falls, the Lower Suspension Bridge is crowded with spectators. (Sherman Zavitz Collection)

One of two men who had been stranded on a scow caught on the rocks not far above the Horseshoe Falls is rescued by breeches buoy on August 7, 1918. The other man was also brought to safety. The scow, now quite rusted, still remains. (Niagara Falls Public Library)

It's October 24, 1901, and Annie Edson Taylor has just become the first person to go over the Falls in a barrel. She had to be sawed out of her barrel and now, bruised and in shock, is being helped ashore. The American Falls are in the background. (Niagara Falls Public Library)

Two Native American hunters survey the scene in this hauntingly beautiful engraving by artist Thomas Cole, entitled *A Distant View of the Falls of Niagara*. There is no other sign of human activity. (*Niagara Park Illustrated*, Sherman Zavitz Collection)

Niagara Falls as seen from above the Whirlpool Rapids in the 1870s. The Falls are about 12,000 years old. During that time they have moved seven miles (11km) upstream from their birthplace. In the process, they have carved out the Niagara Gorge. (*Niagara Park Illustrated*, Sherman Zavitz Collection)

An artist's portrayal of an early attempt at illuminating the Falls. (*Niagara Park Illustrated,* Sherman Zavitz Collection)

The Horseshoe Falls as seen from the road down the side of the Gorge that leads to the ferry landing. The illustration dates to the early 1880s. (*Niagara Park Illustrated*, Sherman Zavitz Collection)

Relaxing in Queen Victoria Park about 1900. The trough at the base of the tree contains piped-in spring water. Several common cups are available for visitors' use. (*Niagara The Majestic*, Sherman Zavitz Collection)

A pathway in Dufferin Islands, as seen around 1900. (*Niagara The Majestic*, Sherman Zavitz Collection)

A 1908 advertisement for the second Clifton Hotel, which had opened two years earlier. The first Clifton Hotel (known as the Clifton House) had been built in 1833 and was destroyed by fire in 1898. (Sherman Zavitz Collection)

This dramatic engraving shows the Cantilever Bridge, a railway span that was used from 1883 to 1925, when it was replaced with an arch-style bridge. The Falls are in the distance. (*A New Guide to Niagara Falls*, Sherman Zavitz Collection)

Intrepid travellers walk behind the Horseshoe or Canadian Falls in this 1880s illustration. The experience was often referred to as "going behind the sheet." (*A New Guide to Niagara Falls*, Sherman Zavitz Collection)

This photo of the Canadian shore was taken from Goat Island in 1879. The large building at the far right was Thomas Barnett's Niagara Falls Museum located where Queen Victoria Place is now. The museum had been built in 1859–60 and was a prominent attraction for many years. The building with the cupola, just left of centre, was Table Rock House, which dated to 1855. A portion of the Horseshoe Falls can be seen at the extreme left. (Niagara Parks Archives)

At one time it was possible to pitch your tent directly overlooking the Horseshoe Falls and upper rapids of the Niagara River. This scene, from the late 1920s, shows the Falls View Tourist Camp in an area that now has a number of high-rise hotels. (Sherman Zavitz Collection)

A lone car makes its way along the roadway through Queen Victoria Park in this photo from 1920. The double tracks of the International Railway Company (Great Gorge Route) can be seen, along with Ramblers Rest, an observation shelter overlooking the Falls and Gorge. Ramblers Rest still stands. (Sherman Zavitz Collection)

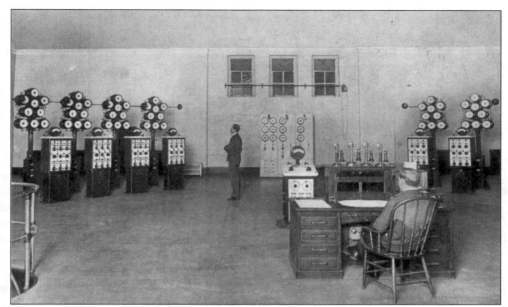

An interesting look at the control room of the Ontario Power Company in 1908. The company's generating plant was located right beside the Niagara River close to the base of the Horseshoe Falls. (Sherman Zavitz Collection)

With the Horseshoe Falls in the background, this old photo from the 1870s looks down on Table Rock House built by Niagara entrepreneur Saul Davis in 1855. It was replaced by the current Table Rock House in 1926. (Sherman Zavitz Collection)

Posing in front of a studio backdrop, this trio of young ladies proudly wear their finest in an era when elaborate hats were the norm. (Sherman Zavitz Collection)

The first European to see Niagara Falls was Father Louis Hennepin, a French-speaking priest who had been born in what is now Belgium. He arrived at the Falls on December 7, 1678, and was greatly impressed, describing the cataracts as "a vast and prodigious cadence of water which falls down after a surprising and astonishing manner insomuch that the universe does not afford its parallel."

Back in Europe, Hennepin wrote an account of his North American travels and adventures. Published in 1697, both this drawing of Niagara Falls and a written description appeared in the book. A best seller, the book gave Europeans their first knowledge of Niagara Falls. (Sherman Zavitz Collection)

These four prints depict the area around the Horseshoe (Canadian) Falls in the early 1860s. Above: Looking down on the Horseshoe Falls (Sherman Zavitz Collection)

Table Rock and Table Rock House (Sherman Zavitz Collection)

The Niagara River just below the Horseshoe Falls. The original Clifton Hotel is in the distance. (Sherman Zavitz Collection)

The Horseshoe Falls in winter (Sherman Zavitz Collection)

William Henry Bartlett's view of the Falls from near the Clifton House Hotel dates to the late 1830s. (Sherman Zavitz Collection)

Henry Bellini performed on a tightrope across the Niagara Gorge near the Falls during the summer of 1873. Here he is seen traveling across his rope, balancing pole in hand. (Sherman Zavitz Collection)

The Clifton House was Niagara Falls's premier nineteenth century hotel. Here we see it in the 1870s. On the left is Clifton Hill, now the well-known Street of Fun. (Sherman Zavitz Collection)

This 1870s look at the Falls from the Canadian side shows the first Upper Suspension Bridge, which had opened in 1869. Note the zigzag fence in the foreground. (Sherman Zavitz Collection)

During the early years of the twentieth century, having your picture taken in a photographer's studio with a backdrop of the Falls was a popular way to remember your visit. The American Falls are at the left; the Canadian Falls are in the distance. (Sherman Zavitz Collection)

Five
Whirpool Rapids, Whirlpool & Glen

A portion of the Whirlpool Rapids, one of the deadliest stretches of whitewater in the world, as seen around 1900. This is the narrowest section of the Niagara River. Here the water is squeezed into a narrow rock-strewn channel just slightly over 300 feet (91m) wide. In addition, the river drops about 60 feet (18m) in less than half a mile. On the left is one of the Great Gorge Route electric line cars. (*Niagara The Majestic*, Sherman Zavitz Collection)

The Whirlpool as it appeared about 1900. During normal flow, the river's water rush-es into the pool with such force that it is carried past the outlet. It then circulates count-er-clockwise around the basin. As the water approaches the pool's entrance, it is cut off by the incoming stream. Hydrostatic pressure builds up from behind, forcing the water down under the incoming stream in order to reach the outlet. (*Niagara The Majestic*, Sherman Zavitz Collection)

This dramatic engraving of the Whirlpool Rapids appeared in *Picturesque Canada* in 1894. (Sherman Zavitz Collection)

A brooding sky adds to the graphic appeal of this drawing showing the Whirlpool Rapids, as published in 1894. (*Picturesque Canada*, Sherman Zavitz Collection)

On the path to the Whirlpool. (*Picturesque Canada*, Sherman Zavitz Collection)

THE WHIRLPOOL,
From American side.

Visitors at the edge of the Whirlpool, looking across to the Canadian side, 1880s.
(*Picturesque Canada*, Sherman Zavitz Collection)

A view from the 1880s showing the Niagara River just above the Whirlpool. The elaborate waterwheel was designed by Leander Colt. It was used as part of the mechanism that powered an incline railway the Colt family had built down the side of the Gorge. (*Picturesque Canada*, Sherman Zavitz Collection)

IN NIAGARA GLEN, NIAGARA FALLS, CANADIAN SIDE.

The photos on the next four pages, all dating to around 1910, were taken in the Glen. One of the prettiest and most interesting areas along the length of the Niagara Gorge, the Glen is truly a geological delight. Here, about 8,000 years ago, a single Falls split into two streams. (Sherman Zavitz Collection)

Pebbly Beach, Niagara Glen, Niagara Falls, Canada.

The Niagara Glen is still a popular destination for today's visitors..

Hanging Rock, Niagara Glen, Niagara Falls, Canada.

LAND OF CANADA THE MAPLE

A pretty spot in Niagara Glen, Niagara Fa

Niagara Falls, Great Gorge Route, Niagara Glen, a resting pavilion.

NIAGARA GLEN, CANADA.

Waiting for Car in Heights above Niagara Glen. Niagara Falls, Canada.

Waiting for the electric line cars above the Glen around 1910. (Sherman Zavitz Collection)

Six

Queenston

Flanked by two cannons, a group of visitors enjoy the view of the lower Niagara River from atop Queenston Heights around 1910. (Sherman Zavitz Collection)

The stunning view from Queenston Heights has captured the attention of many artists over the years. This depiction was done in the 1880s. Note the couple on a bench near the lower left corner, the sailing ship at the Queenston Wharf, and the remains of the first Lewiston-Queenston Suspension Bridge near the right side of the engraving. (*Picturesque Canada*, Sherman Zavitz Collection)

A view of Queenston Heights and Brock's Monument from the Niagara River, circa 1910. Queenston Heights Park surrounds Brock's Monument on top of the Niagara Escarpment. The park offers many recreational facilities such as picnic pavilions, a wading pool and tennis courts. Queenston Heights Park is at the southern end of the 460-mile-long (740km) Bruce Trail, which follows the escarpment to Tobermory at the northern end of the Bruce Peninsula. (Sherman Zavitz Collection)

Battle of Queenstown Heights, October 13th, 1812.

The Battle of Queenston Heights on October 13, 1812, was a key victory for Canada during the first year of the War of 1812. The British, Canadians and their Native allies were commanded by the charismatic and capable Major General Isaac Brock. During the opening stages of the battle, as Brock led a small detachment up the side of the Heights to dislodge an American position, he was killed by an enemy sharp-shooter. Although this painting has various inaccuracies, it does manage to convey some of the drama of the moment as Isaac Brock, mortally wounded, lies on the battlefield. Although Brock became the hero of the battle, the victory was actually achieved later in the day by Major General Roger Hale Sheaffe. (Sherman Zavitz Collection)

This dramatic engraving of Brock's Monument on Queenston Heights dates to 1860. The imposing monument, 190 feet (58m) high, was constructed between 1853 and 1856. It was dedicated on the 47th anniversary of the Battle of Queenston Heights, October 13, 1859. The small monument in the foreground marks the approximate location where General Brock died. (*Our Own Country*, Sherman Zavitz Collection)

Memorial Stone placed by King Edward VII. when Prince of Wales, 1860, Queenston, Canada

THIS STONE
WAS PLACED BY HIS ROYAL HIGHNESS
ALBERT EDWARD PRINCE OF WALES
ON 18 SEPTEMBER 1860

This stone, marking the approximate site where Isaac Brock fell during the Battle of Queenston Heights, was dedicated by the Prince of Wales (later King Edward VII) in 1860. The photo dates to about 1910. (Sherman Zavitz Collection)

This early twentieth century view is looking south into the Village of Queenston with the Heights and Brock's Monument in the distance. (Sherman Zavitz Collection)

This is what Laura Secord's home in Queenston looked like in 1913, one hundred years after her famous walk. By this time, her former residence had been considerably altered. It was in the early morning of June 22, 1813, that Laura set out from this house and walked some 20 miles to the west to warn a British outpost of an impending American attack. Her information helped the British and their Native allies prepare for and win what became known as the Battle of Beaver Dams. In 1971 the Laura Secord Company, famous for its chocolates, restored the house to its original appearance. It is now owned by The Niagara Parks Commission. (Sherman Zavitz Collection)

The Lewiston-Queenston Suspension Bridge around 1908. The view is looking west towards Queenston Heights. This bridge opened in 1899 and was used until 1962, when the present span was opened. (Sherman Zavitz Collection)

For many years steamboats regularly sailed between Queenston, Niagara-on-the-Lake and Toronto. Here, a large crowd at Queenston in the early 1920s awaits the arrival of the *Cayuga*. From the Queenston dock, passengers could travel by streetcar into Niagara Falls. (Sherman Zavitz Collection)

A steamboat departs the Queenston Dock about 1910. (Sherman Zavitz Collection)

Although largely in ruins by the time this photo was taken around 1920, back in 1824 this building had been the home of William Lyon Mackenzie. A political agitator who campaigned for government reform, Mackenzie first published his influential newspaper, *The Colonial Advocate,* in this house. Now restored, the building is owned by The Niagara Parks Commission. It is the home of the Mackenzie Heritage Printery and Newspaper Museum. (Sherman Zavitz Collection)

This was the original Queenston Heights Restaurant, which was built in 1900. It was replaced by the present restaurant in 1940. (Sherman Zavitz Collection)

The Queenston-Chippawa Generating Plant at Queenston as it looked in the early 1920s. Now called the Adam Beck Generating Station No. 1, this plant opened in December 1921 as the largest hydroelectric generating plant in the world. Over the following nine years, the facility was expanded to house a total of 10 generators. (Sherman Zavitz Collection)

A view of Queenston Village and the lower Niagara River as drawn by W.H. Bartlett in 1838. At the left is the original Brock's Monument. Built in 1824, it was destroyed by a terrorist in 1840. (*Queenston Heights Park*, Sherman Zavitz Collection)

This intriguing drawing was made on birch bark by Elizabeth Simcoe. She was the wife of John Graves Simcoe, the first Lieutenant Governor of Upper Canada (now Ontario) from 1791 to 1796. The scene is Queenston with the Heights rising in the background. The buildings along the waterfront were barracks for the Queen's Rangers. (*Hulbert's The Niagara River*)

Seven
Niagara-on-the-Lake

McFarland's Landing on the Niagara River, a short distance upriver from the McFarland House, circa 1860. (Niagara Historical Society and Museum)

The McFarland House has been a landmark building along the lower Niagara River since its construction by John McFarland in 1800. In the basement, a number of the original tree trunk ceiling beams (some with the bark still on them) may still be seen. Used as a hospital during the War of 1812, the house was left with considerable damage. Soon repaired, the house remained in the McFarland family until the late 1930s. Now owned by The Niagara Parks Commission, it is open to the public during the summer months. This winter view is from the early twentieth century. (Niagara Historical Society and Museum)

A panoramic view of the mouth of the Niagara River as it flows into Lake Ontario. The drawing, dating to around 1890, was made from the ramparts of Fort George, then in ruins. (*Picturesque Canada*, Sherman Zavitz Collection)

The Masonic Hall, Niagara Lodge No. 2 in Niagara-on-the-Lake, as seen around 1915. This lodge was well organized by the early 1790s and met at an earlier Free Masons' Hall on this site. The building in the photo is believed to have been constructed, at least in part, from the rubble of the town after its destruction during the War of 1812. It was eventually purchased by the Masons who then returned to the site of their original home.It is still being used. (Sherman Zavitz Collection)

Two views of the Niagara-on-the-Lake wharf from 1907. Here ships on the Queenston, Niagara-on-the-Lake, Toronto run met Michigan Central Railway trains that could take passengers to Niagara Falls, Fort Erie and Buffalo. (Sherman Zavitz Collection)

STEAMER CHIPPEWA AT WHARF
NIAGARA ON THE LAKE.

A wider view of the Niagara-on-the-Lake wharf and harbour. Lake Ontario is in the distance. (Sherman Zavitz Collection)

A royal intersection – the corner of Queen and King Streets, circa 1910. James Connolly's Jewellery Store is on the left. At the bottom of the picture, the Michigan Central Railway tracks may be seen along King Street. (Sherman Zavitz Collection)

A steamboat glides into the Niagara River in this picture-perfect scene from 1905. Fort Niagara is in the distance. Built by the French in 1726, it is on the New York State side of the river. (Sherman Zavitz Collection)

For many decades the Queen's Royal was the most prestigious hotel in Niagara-on-the-Lake. It was built in 1868 at the mouth of the Niagara River overlooking Lake Ontario. The Queen's Royal quickly became a summer holiday mecca for well-to-do tourists from both sides of the border. Publicity for the hotel in 1897 enthused, "The magnificent suites of apartments, broad piazzas, extensive lawns and cuisine marked by delicious English and French cooking, makes this charming summer place justly celebrated." The hotel was torn down in the 1930s and a namesake park now occupies the site. These five photos, all dating to the early years of the twentieth century, show the Queen's Royal along with one of its verandahs, the dining room, rotunda and a guest room. (Sherman Zavitz Collection)

ROTUNDA, QUEEN'S ROYAL HOTEL.
NIAGARA-ON-THE-LAKE.

Verandah, Queen's Royal Hotel,
Niagara-on-the-Lake, Ont., Canada

Cavalry Manoeuvres, Niagara Camp

Niagara-on-the-Lake has had a long connection with the military. Most of the large area now generally called the Commons was set aside by the British Government as a military reserve during the very early years of settlement in the area. Beginning in 1872, this was the site each summer of Camp Niagara for the training of militia. The camp was an extremely busy place during both World Wars. Militia training continued here on a reduced scale until 1967 when it was relocated further west to the Department of National Defence property along Lake Ontario. These 5 photos offer a look at Camp Niagara during the early 1900s.
(Sherman Zavitz Collection)

A church parade-1907. (Sherman Zavitz Collection)

Cavalry line, World War I. (Sherman Zavitz Collection)

Premier Borden Reviewing Over-seas Forces at Niagara Camp.

Prime Minister Robert Borden, with his hat raised in salute, reviewing the troops, in training during the First World War. (Sherman Zavitz Collection)

Throwing grenades from the trenches, First World War. (Sherman Zavitz Collection)

Inoculation at Old Navy Hall, Niagara Camp.

Soldiers about to head overseas during the First World War were inoculated at historic Navy Hall. Built in 1815, this structure replaced an earlier building, constructed at the time of the American Revolution, which was destroyed during the War of 1812. (Sherman Zavitz Collection)

A Draft for Over-seas, Embarking for the Front.

Packed with soldiers, a ship departs Niagara-on-the-Lake on the first leg of a journey that will ultimately take the men to the European front. Quite possibly some of them would never see their homes again. (Sherman Zavitz Collection)

View from Fort Mississauga, showing part of
C. E. F. Camp and Niagara River,
Niagara-on-the-Lake, Canada.

During the First World War, the Niagara-on-the-Lake Golf Course (established in 1875) had to temporarily vacate its property to allow for an extension of Camp Niagara. This photo, taken from Fort Mississauga, shows the camp and the Niagara River. The golf course returned home in 1920. (Sherman Zavitz Collection)

A section of Camp Niagara during the Second World War. The dining tents are at the left. (Sherman Zavitz Collection)

The winter quarters at Camp Niagara during the Second World War. (Sherman Zavitz Collection)

A lone piper plays at twilight amid the tents of Camp Niagara during the Second World War. (Sherman Zavitz Collection)

Fort Mississauga, as sketched by Benson Lossing around 1860. The fort was constructed by the British in 1814 to replace Fort George, which the Americans had largely destroyed during their evacuation of the site the previous December. (*Lossing's Pictorial Field Book of the War of 1812*)

"The Taking of Fort George." This engraving appeared in a Philadelphia magazine in 1817. It is the only known nearly contemporary depiction of the battle of May 27, 1813, during which the Americans captured the fort. The drawing was made from out in Lake Ontario, looking towards the mouth of the Niagara River. In the foreground, the U.S. squadron bombards British positions. The small boats are carrying troops towards shore. Fort Niagara is at the far left, Fort George on the other side of the Niagara River and the Town of Niagara (Niagara-on-the-Lake) with its lighthouse, is in the middle. The lighthouse dated to 1804. It was dismantled in 1814 so its brick could be used for the construction of Fort Mississauga on the same site. (Niagara Historical Society and Museum)

Fishing on the Niagara River at Niagara-on-the-Lake in the 1890s. (Sherman Zavitz Collection)

A tranquil scene along the Niagara River near Niagara-on-the-Lake, circa 1896. (Sherman Zavitz Collection)

The Oban Inn in the mid-1890s. This long-established popular inn was destroyed by fire on Christmas Day, 1992. Within a year a new inn, virtually identical in appearance to the original, arose on the same site. Diners whose Christmas dinner had been interrupted because of the fire were invited back to finish their dinner on Christmas Day, 1993. (Sherman Zavitz Collection)

The Niagara House at the corner of King and Picton Streets as it looked in 1904. This is now part of the Prince of Wales Hotel. (Sherman Zavitz Collection)

The home and farm of Willis Jackson along the Niagara River near Niagara-on-the-Lake, circa 1904. The large house still stands. (Sherman Zavitz Collection)

Construction of Fort George began in 1796. Largely destroyed by the end of the War of 1812, it was reconstructed in 1937 and is now a National Historic Site administered by Parks Canada. This photo dates to around 1900 and shows the fort's powder magazine, the only building still standing at that time. (*Niagara The Majestic*, Sherman Zavitz Collection)

An early view of Fort George from the American side of the Niagara River. (Niagara Historical Society and Museum)

The Elliott House,
Niagara-on-the-Lake,
Ontario, Canada.

This building, which dates to the mid-1830s, was originally known as the Whale Inn. Now a private home for many years, its prominent location at the foot of King Street beside the Niagara River has made it a landmark building. (Niagara Historical Society and Museum)